Never
Alone

MABEL HASSAN

Trafford
PUBLISHING

Order this book online at www.trafford.com
or email orders@trafford.com

Most Trafford titles are also available at major online book retailers.

Printed in the United States of America.

ISBN: 978-1-4251-1961-4 (sc)

Trafford rev. 06/30/2012

 www.trafford.com

North America & international
toll-free: 1 888 232 4444 (USA & Canada)
phone: 250 383 6864 ✦ fax: 812 355 4082

CONTENTS

CONTENTS

DEDICATION

This book is dedicated to God almighty and to my late beloved mother.

A CHILD IS BORN

Carole had been childless for 11 years and all hope of having a child had disappeared. She was the second child of Mr and Mrs Brian. While growing up her dad who was a teacher refuse to educate his girls, saying, "A woman's education ends in the kitchen." He wanted her to get married at the age of 15 but Carole insisted she wanted to go to school. Her decision infuriated her family who turned their backs on her leaving her financially to continue her studies.

But Carole wasn't to be denied. She was a hard worker not a quitter. She decided to ventured deep into the forest to pick up some palm nuts, where she picked a great number of them, then headed to the market to sell them to traders. The money she got from her sales was used by Carole to register herself at school.

Carole wanted to be a nurse but she had struggled financially to fund her primary and secondary school education. She did, however, fell in love with a handsome guy called Victor. Victor was the only child of his parents. His dad died when he was born leaving his mum to take care of him. His mum was wealthy; she owned a chain of supermarkets in Lag. He lacked nothing in his childhood.

While in courtship, Victor paid for Carole's nursing school fees and saw her through her nursing education and eventually got married. The marriage began well enough, after two years, they went on a visit to an hospital for check-ups, they were told by their physician that they were medically ok to have children. They would simply have to be patient and hopefully have children when the right time comes.

Mary, Victor's mum, was a spiteful and aggressive woman. From time to time she would often visit the couple but one occasion she arrived to find Carole alone.

"Carole, where is my son?" his mother demanded.

"He's at work," she replied.

"I see. So all you do is to sit at home, or go out and buy shoes, necklaces, and whatever else, all at my son's expense, you little witch! And you can't even give me a child. I want grandchildren, but all I have is you, a barren, childless witch of a woman".

Carole was astonished by her remarks and began to cry. "I'm a woman, I have what it takes to bear a child and my health is okay, it's not my fault I can't have a child of my own" she cried. Her mother-in-law stormed out of the house leaving Carole feeling devastated.

When Victor arrived home, his wife told him all that happened; he couldn't believe his ears. But things were to get worse for Carole when two weeks later her mother in-law came back to the house and sent Carole packing, leaving her with no food or clothes.

She managed to rent a flat and stayed there for just over a year and finally found a man who accepted her for who she was. However, Daniel, had had many children from his polygamous relationships and had to cater for those children's needs as well as his own.

Carole met Daniel at a friend's party. He was lonely and needed a partner for a dance; he approached Carole who at first refused but later decided to accept his offer. As they were dancing, Daniel leaned slightly forward to kiss her and she refused at first but later succumbed to his advances. They started dating and two months later Daniel expressed his desire to further their relationship.

They often had dinner together but on one evening, Daniel gave an engagement ring to the waiter, telling him to put it in Carole's ice cream. "Madam," said the waiter, "your dessert." She put a spoonful of ice cream into her mouth and bit something hard.

"What's this?" she said in amazement after she'd removed the ring from her mouth.

Mr Daniel smiled broadly, took the ring from her, knelt down and said, "Carole, will you marry me?" Carole was taken by surprise, lost for words but finally she managed to say yes and the wedding went ahead. Two months after the happy occasion, Carole discovered she was pregnant.

Eight months and three weeks into the pregnancy Carole was sitting in the living room when suddenly she had a sharp pain which, continued until she could no longer cope so she called for help. She was rushed to the hospital where she had a girl called Ruth. Carole was happy because she now had little one, her joy as a woman has been fulfilled.

Ruth grew up quickly, at three month she had her first tooth. She was dark-skin and had long black hair. She was very smart and knew ways of obtaining food from other children even though they were older than her. Ruth's mother Carole found out she was two months pregnant, she was very excited about the news, "the days of my bareness is over", she said.

Ruth began to walk at the age of seven months. The neighbours continued to bear a grudge against the child, told her mum to push her down, claiming that it was too early for Ruth to walk. As the child grew she responded to the hostility by protecting herself with her tiny teeth. A month after her first birthday, Carole was rushed to the hospital to give birth; the children were left at home knowing they would have to contend with the neighbours. But just three days later Carole came home with another tiny baby. She called him Jude because he was born in the month of June.

Meanwhile her parents quarrelled all the time over her kid brother. Jude was suffering from an eye problem and the doctor told his parents that he should be taken to an eye specialist for surgery as Jude will need surgery to see properly again. During this time Ruth's dad was becoming an aggressive person; he would shout at her mother and end up beating her.

The day arrived for Ruth's mum to take her little brother to the hospital. She packed some of her belongings because she didn't know when she would be coming back home. However, she promised Ruth and her sibling she would be coming home soon. Ruth's dad gave her 300 naira to care for the child, and she set out on the long journey.

It was a rainy day with thunder and lightening and most people were home except Ruth who was playing in the rain with her half brothers and sisters. Suddenly, her dad appeared and said, "Hey, come here, take yourselves indoors and dry yourselves."

"No!" replied Ruth's sister, adding, "I want to play in the rain."

He looked at her, his eyes red with anger. If he didn't get his own way he could turn violent.

He had decided to leave with the children. He packed everyone's belongings, and took the children from Lag to Del. This is where Ruth, her brother and two sisters grew up. They no longer had a mother to care for them.

In the village in Del, Ruth and her siblings were known as bastards. The children in the village would call them names and beat them up whenever they walked by. Ruth later found out why her dad had told the villagers that her mum left them all when Ruth was nine months old. She had become a prostitute and was eventually murdered and buried by the riverside. Other mothers warned their children not to play with Ruth and her siblings, saying that they were evil, bastard children.

One hot afternoon, Ruth was walking down the road to buy some coconut rice and stew. She crossed the road and found herself face to face with Sam, the village bully. He was 12 years old, fat, wide-mouthed and very strong. Sam was the only boy in his family, his parents having had him after nine girls, his parents and sisters spoilt him; he didn't even know how to clean his teeth let alone bath himself. All the children in the village feared him as he would beat everyone, even his friends, and he wasn't afraid of those older than him. He would steal and break into people houses and his parents would just laugh and say, "Leave him, he is only a child."

When Ruth saw him, her heart leapt and she shuddered. She wished the ground would open up and swallow her. But there was no escape. She began to walk faster but he laughed at her and shouted, "Hey, you, idiot. I order you to stand there!" She knew he was talking to her but didn't react to his provocation. Again he demanded that she should stop. She continued to walk, so he began to chase her. He caught up with her and pushed her with his fat hand.

Ruth landed on the ground. "What have I done?" she asked. He spat on her and began to beat her. She was too afraid to fight back, so he bit her mercilessly causing her to scream out loud in pain. As he continued to beat her, Ruth's brother appeared, carrying a belt and used it to hit him and knock him to the ground.

"You big fat bully, are you trying to kill my sister?" The bully screamed and pleaded for mercy. Her brother helped her up and made sure she was okay. Ruth pulled the bully's leg and he fell to the ground. As he did so, passers-by stopped to watch the fight; her brother put some sand in his mouth and she joined in by biting every part of the bully's body.

All the children gathered round and laughed at the bully. He was the village terror, everyone was happy he had been beaten. The next day, his mum, dad, and his nine sisters brought him to their house and told Ruth's father his children had been walking past their son and attacked him. They wanted medication for his wounds.

Not surprising, her dad was very disappointed with her and her brothers. He treated the bully, gave him some medication and advised his parents to take him home so that he can have some rest. Ruth and her brothers were very happy; at last they could walk round the village without worrying about someone attacking them.

Ruth and her siblings weren't liked by the majority of their neighbours. Despite their honesty to their loved ones, their obedience and the errands they performed, the villagers still hated them because they had no mother. Mothers often warned their children not to play with them, calling them evil, even at school; the teachers didn't like other children sitting or mixing with them. They were treated like lepers.

Ruth found a friend in Tina who treated her differently from the others. They attended the same school, played together, ate together and studied together. Tina was an only child and her parents accepted whoever their daughter accepted. She had an aunty who lived in Lagos with two other relatives of hers. Her auntie's name was Carole, she had been married but the husband had taken the children and ran away, her uncle's Jimmy and James stayed at home all day, they had no job, no wife nor children. All they did was cause problems in the house and criticise Tina for every little thing she did.

One day, Tina and Ruth were playing outside Tina's house when a woman with a dark complexion and long hair came into the compound, carrying a large travelling bag. Suddenly, all the children playing outside started shouting, "Aunty Carole!" Within the twinkling of an eye she was surrounded by the excited children. Tina offered to carry her bag and others threw their arms around her. Ruth had never seen the other kids so happy.

The woman walked up to Ruth and said in a very soft and angelic voice, "Little one, what is your name?"

"I don't talk to strangers," she replied, "because my dad told me not to." The woman smiled at her and walked away.

That evening Tina came round to Ruth's house and Ruth asked her who the woman was and Tina said she it was her Aunt Carole who lived in Lagos. "She's a nurse," Tina added, "and lives in a very big mansion. She has three children, now taken away, and she said they look like you and your brother, and she thinks you are her daughter."

Ruth laughed and said, "What makes her think my brothers and I are her children?"

One evening Ruth and Tina were playing outside when Aunty Carole walked up to them and said, "In two weeks time it will be my daughter's birthday." Then she began to sob. "Ruth, where are you? Your dad took you from me. God, please help me find my children."

Ruth was touched by Carole's tears and said, "Aunty, don't worry, you will find your children… it's funny though, thinking about it."

"What do you mean?" said Carole.

"My brother and I… our birthdays fall upon the same days as your children! Come to think of it, how come they bear the same names as us?"

Carole thought for a while. "I wish I could have another child." Uncle Jimmy, Carole's brother said, "I know a man who can help. Ruth's dad is a doctor and he helps women that are childless."

Two days later Carole and her brother showed up at Ruth's house and knocked on the door. Ruth asked who it was and when she opened the door, Aunty Carole was standing right in front of her on the doorstep.

"What do you want?" Ruth asked.

She replied, "I want to see your dad."

"My dad's not at home," she replied. But as soon as Ruth's dad heard the conversation at the door he called to Ruth to let them in.

Ruth's dad entered the room and as soon as he saw Carole, he shouted, "What do you want!"

Carole was surprised at his reaction and said, "Daniel, is this you or your spirit? What have I done to deserve this, where are my children?"

"Who are you, and what do you want, and which daughter are you talking about?"

As the shouting grew worse, the whole villagers started to gather. Ruth's sisters rushed out of the house and immediately they saw Carole they shouted, "Mum, Mummy!"

Carole's hands were wide open; she cried and embraced the children before asking, "Where is your little sister, Ruth?"

On hearing this, Ruth was shocked. So her mother wasn't dead, her dad had lied to her. She couldn't take it in and asked her dad if Aunty Carole really was her mother. "No," he said, "take no notice of her."

"Carole said, "Thank you, Jesus, for letting me see this day.

Ruth asked her dad again and again if that was her mother or if she was lying.

Finally, her father gave in and admitted she had left her when she was six-months old. "Yes, she is your mother, Ruth."

Ruth fell down and cried and Carole held her daughter close to her. But Ruth wasn't happy; she wanted to know why her mother had left her at such a young age.

"I didn't leave you," she explained, "your dad took you all away while I was at the hospital with your brother Jude who I'd taken in for an eye operation. By the time I returned from the hospital all my things were outside the house. That was when I started the journey looking for all of you and during the process I lost your little brother Jude. But I'm just so happy to have found you all."

It was an amazing day for Ruth. She had found her mum and discovered that her best friend was in fact her cousin. She spent all day trying to find out more about her mother. "I'll be going back to Lag soon," she said, "and then I'll be coming back." Ruth was glad to hear this but later expressed her anger with her dad for having lied to her all this years.

Three days later it was Ruth's birthday. Her mum returned from Lag just in time for the birthday party and brought birthday cards, clothes and various gifts. She then took her daughter out shopping. Ruth's birthday party was one of her best birthday party's ever. She was delighted she had found her mother and to make it even better all the children in the village were present to celebrate with her. She was no longer thought of as bastard and considered evil. That was now all behind her.

After the party, Ruth's dad called for her mum, knelt down and begged for her forgiveness and for her to come back. Carole told him he was forgiven but would never go back to him as his wife.

Ruth was now happier than she had been for a long time. It felt great to have a mother and she introduced her to all her friends. The time came for her mum to go back to Lag but she promised to come back to take her daughter.

A few days after Ruth's mum had left, her dad called her and said, "My daughter, you are now eight years old and as tradition demands all the daughters of the village must be circumcised, now or when they are about to get married so that they will not have been a flirt before meeting their husband. Ruth was scared because she had seen people who had experienced it and it was a very painful procedure. She begged her dad not to circumcise her till she was old enough to get married. Her intention was to run away from home when she was about to get married but her dad said within two weeks after the circumcision all would be okay.

Ruth was in her room doing her schoolwork when a number of women came to the house and asked after her dad. She told her he had gone out so one of the women asked her to come with them to the sitting room. She got up and followed them and saw there were gifts, drinks and food everywhere and when she asked what it was all about, she was told they were celebrating.

Ruth and her siblings ate and drank with them and one of them asked Ruth to follow her to her house because she had something to give to her dad. She put on her shoes and followed the woman. They walked for about two miles and finally reached the woman's house where she was surprised to see her dad. "Dad," she said, "what are you doing here?"

"Today," he replied, is your day. We are here to celebrate." Suddenly, four men came into the house and carried Ruth into the sitting room. She shouted for help but her dad didn't come to help her. One of the men took off her clothes while the women she saw earlier came in with blades, water, scissors and a white piece of cloth. Ruth now realised what was about to happen to her. She cried for help and struggled but the men held her down; she was held so tightly that she could not move any part of her body. One of the women brought out the blades and with the men holding her very tight, Ruth was circumcised. When they had finished, Ruth was helpless, in pain, and lying on the ground with blood all over her. It was an extremely painful and brutal experience.

The women took her home where she found her dad sitting with some elders in the living room, drinking and chatting. Immediately they saw Ruth they all started to sing and dance. Then the women led her into her room where she was to remain for the next two weeks during which the wound would heal. Meanwhile everyone continued to celebrate.

Ruth was initial dismay and bitter, she was not happy with her dad so she kept her distance and refused to speak to her dad. After a while she had a change of heart because the deed had been done and not talking to him wouldn't turn back the clock, so she started talking to her dad and he was appreciative. However,

Ruth advised all her friends to avoid circumcision if possible as it was so painful.

One morning, Ruth's half-sister Janet who lived in Lag came to visit and said she would be leaving the next day. Ruth's dad asked if Ruth would like to go with Janet to Lag to spend the rest of her holiday, "Ruth was delighted and said yes" she was delighted at the thought she would see her mum again thinking Lag is a small place where everybody knows everybody.

After a long distance travel, they arrived at Lag in the evening feeling very tired, and as they had already had lunch on the way they went straight to bed. At 6 o' clock the next morning, her sister Janet woke Ruth up. "Ruth," she said, "wake up, there is no food or money, please will you take some peppers to the market, the profit will be use for the day's meal." Ruth got up and without taking a wash; she carried the pepper on her head down to the market. She went into the street to hawk and by 2 pm she had sold all the pepper and headed home. When she returned she found that her half sister Janet and her daughter were eating, Ruth was happy to see that they had cooked something before she got home. She greeted her, washed her hands and sat down to join them.

She wasn't prepared for what followed. Janet shouted, "Where do you think you are! In your father's house or your mother's house? You will go back to the market to sell all these tomatoes, young lady, and make sure you sell all of them, if you don't then don't come home. Ruth was shocked. She begged her to let her eat, bathe and rest before going back to the market but Janet pounced on her, beat her and forced her to carry a tray of pineapples to sell. Ruth now realised she wasn't welcomed in the house.

On the road, she looked everywhere for her mum but she was nowhere to be found. She believed that as Lag was a small place she would easily find her but Lag was more crowded than she'd expected. Eventually, she managed to sell some pineapples. She was hungry and thirsty so she returned home at past five that evening.

Ruth was hoping to eat and have a shower as soon as she got home but little did she know that she would be facing something quite different. She opened the door to find her sister in the sitting room. She gave her the money she had earned from the market, hoping her sister would be happy at what she had done for her. But Janet slapped her on the face and said, "You stupid girl, you did not sell everything I gave you, what will happen to the rest, do you want them to spoil?"

She beat her with a cane, swore at her, insulted her mum, and went inside the house to bring out all her dirty clothes to be washed. Ruth carried the clothes away and as she washed them she started to sing a song:

'Give me joy in my heart, keep me moving, give me joy in my heart. I pray give me joy in my heart, keep me moving, keep me moving till the end of day, sing Hosanna, sing Hosanna, sing Hosanna to the King of Kings..'

The holiday was now over and Ruth began to pack all her luggage, happy to be leaving. However, her niece saw her packing and ran to tell her mum. Janet, her sister, came and asked why she was packing and where she intended going. "I want to go back to my dad," she said.

Janet began to swear at her and insulted her mum and dad. Ruth was in tears, Janet jumped on her, took all her clothes and gave them to her daughter Esther. Esther was the only surviving child of Janet. Janet had seven children but they all died during the first year of their life. Esther was a spoilt little brat. She got everything she wanted; she did not know how to clean her teeth never mind bath herself.

Ruth was left with nothing and woke up the next morning with bruises all over her body.

The next day Janet gave Ruth some clothes to wash. When she asked for soap she was told to wash the clothes as they were. So Ruth had no choice but to wash the clothes without soap, later, not surprisingly, found the clothes were not clean. Janet shouted at her: "Come here, stupid girl, black witch, you did not wash the clothes I gave you to! Ruth replied she did wash them, but she had been given no soap. But she continued to shout at her and call her names.

Things didn't get any better. Janet told Ruth to cook dinner and make sure the food wasn't burnt. Unfortunately, Ruth wasn't too good at food preparation as she was only 8 years old but she gave it a go anyway and served it to Janet and her daughter Esther. Then she asked if she could join them at the table but she was given verbal abuse and told she would not be given any food for two days. When Ruth asked why, Janet complained that she hadn't washed the clothes properly and the food hadn't been prepared properly; it had been full of water, pepper and salt. Ruth was devastated when she was told she would not eat for two days because she knew Janet doesn't make empty threats. She felt ravenous with hunger. But despite her increasing weakness she didn't dare mention it.

Nothing changed. She would take Janet's daughter Esther to school, clean the house, and hawk food in the street and market. She drank lots of water and rummaged through waste bins for foods. On the third day, she was sick, weak and hungry. Still, Janet called her and gave her 100 doughnuts to sell. She took the doughnuts and went into the street to sell them but after three hours of hawking, she was very tired and dizzy. Ruth was starving; she ate some of the doughnuts, three of them in fact. But she knew there would be consequences for her when she returned home.

Then she thought of a way of getting the money back for the doughnuts she'd eaten and decided to beg for it. She knew it was either that or there'd be an almighty row when she gets home. So in desperation she started to beg for money. Some of the passers-by gave her loose change while some just walked away. Eventually, Ruth realised it was time she made her way back because her sister had given her three hours to come home. All of them had to have been sold and, of course, Ruth had to hand over all the money from her sale.

She thought about the one naira remaining but decided her sister would not notice so she went home reasonably happy. She arrived home and gave the money to her, before walking outside to wash the dirty dishes. Suddenly she heard someone calling her. "Ruth! Come here, thief, where are you!"

Ruth was shaking and walked quietly and slowly towards her. "The money you gave me is not complete." Ruth wished the ground would open and swallow her up. She could offer no excuse. "Where is my money, you thief?"

She dragged Ruth out of the house, stripped her naked and tied her hands and legs together so she couldn't move, before going into the house and coming out with a cane. She beat her mercilessly then went into the house leaving Ruth lying helplessly on the dusty ground. All the neighbours and their children were watching but were too scared to help because they knew her sister was troublesome.

Next, she came out with a cup full of watering grinded peppers and rubbed the pepper all over Ruth's body. Ruth begged God to take her life. She could not run or touch any part of her body; all she could do was shout and scream for help but no one came to her rescue. Janet took a grinding stone and placed Ruth's right foot on it before hitting her big toe with a stone. Ruth screamed and jumped up. The force caused the rope tied round her to come off and she began to run. But Janet ran after her and hit her backside with a wooden plank. The wooden plank contained nails and the nails sank into her causing patches of blood to appear. By now she was in great pain. Janet looked at her and told her to make sure that in future she did as she was told. And with that she walked away.

The neighbours and passers-by came to Ruth aid and helped lay flat on the floor. Another pulled the wooden plank out of her backside. Besides being in great pain, she was hungry, thirsty and very weak. The neighbours took her to the nearest chemist, treated her wounds and gave her some tablets, after which she was asked to go home. But the neighbours refused to take her home. One of them took her to her house and gave her a hot bath and some food. She stayed for three weeks before finally starting to make a recovery.

But eventually the neighbour became afraid Janet would come seeking a fight so they asked Ruth to go back home. Ruth woke up at six o'clock one morning and decided to go and knock on Janet's door; she knocked but there was no reply so she assumed they were still sleeping. Then she sat on the doorstep with her sore backside, broken toe and wounded body. Janet woke up and saw Ruth on the doorstep and eventually let her in.

Two weeks later, Ruth began to have nightmares and told her sister Janet, who decided Ruth was possessed and took her to her church where she was told Ruth was a witch and would have to be delivered. So she was tied to the doorstep of the church and flogged by members of the congregation and this continued for a week. She thought she was going to die but God restored her and gave her strength. She came back home two weeks later with an aching body and a swollen neck.

SWEET MOTHER

Janet saw that Ruth couldn't move her neck which meant she would be unable to carry the basket on her head and could not sell in the market. Janet tied a black thread round Ruth's neck and said it would ease the pain. A week later, she gave her some bags filled with oil and told her to wash them, again without soap. It was going to be another day of misery. Then something unexpected happened. While Ruth was washing the bags, she heard someone called her name. "Who's calling me?" she said.

"You stupid girl," came the reply. "Who called you? Maybe those witches' friends of yours are here to see you." Ruth walked away slowly. As she bent down she heard someone call her name again. She looked up and there, standing in front of her, was her mother Carole. She thought she was dreaming or in a trance.

Carole said to her, "Come on, Ruth, come to your mum."

Then Ruth realised the voice had been real so she ran to her, hugged her and cried before saying, "Take me with you please, I have been looking everywhere for you. I agreed to come to Lagos so I could see you but I couldn't find you, please take me with you."

Carole looked at her and started to weep. Janet came out and saw Ruth's mum and screamed, "Iyawo! Iyawo! She knocked on a neighbour's door and told them her step-mum was here and they should come out and greet her. The neighbours came out and greeted Ruth's mum warmly. Then they all walked in and gave her a cold drink as it was very hot day.

Later that evening, the neighbours spoke to Ruth's mum in private and told her all about the way Janet had brutally treated Ruth. Carole was in tears and one of them said to her, "You had better take your child. If you don't, then by the time you come back you will find her dead."

Ruth's mum looked at her daughter's injuries and asked her why her toe was swollen and why she had sores on her body. But Ruth was afraid of telling her mum the truth because she thought she might tell Janet. So she decided to say nothing.

That evening her mum prepared some rice and stew and they all ate dinner. During the course of the meal, her mum asked, "Why is Ruth not going to school?"

Janet said, "Ruth does not like school, all she does is sit at home all day and even when she does go, the teachers call home and complain that she steals in class. Carole knew Janet was lying but she kept silent. After they had finished eating, she called Janet and gave her some money for Ruth's school fees. She said she wanted her child to go to school like other children and become someone. Carole called her daughter and told her to make sure she went to school and behave herself.

Janet took the money but instead of using it to pay Ruth's school fees she went to the market and bought more goods for Ruth to sell. When Ruth's mum came back home she asked Janet where her daughter was. Janet confessed and replied that she had told Ruth to go hawking in the market.

"What about her schooling and the money I gave you for her fees?" said her mother.

"I used the money to buy more goods; the profit will be used for Ruth's school fees," came the reply. Her mum said nothing and kept her thoughts to herself.

At 1.30pm the next day, Janet went to see a friend. Ruth's mum decided to take advantage of her absence. She called her daughter, packed all her belongings and told the neighbours they were leaving. The neighbours were pleased for them and agreed it was for the best. They offered Ruth gifts consisting of shoes, clothes and some money then wished them well.

They arrived at Bary late that evening. All the houses were tall and painted in blue and white. They walked for about five minutes until they came to an open estate then walked into a high building. Ruth was amazed when they used the lift as she hadn't been in one before.

They stepped out on the 5th floor. Her mum took out the luggage and opened a door. The house seemed so big inside she thought she was in a palace. There was a large plasma-screen TV and a hi-fi radio system with two loudspeakers. As she wandered around the house, her mum said, "My daughter, welcome home, this is your home now and no one will mistreat you again."

She asked her to sit down but Ruth refused. She was so scared she would stain the sofa, so she chose to remain standing. She was happy, however, to hear her mother say her brother was coming the next day. She missed her brother greatly. Her mum said, "Ruth, I am your mother and you are my daughter, everything in this house is yours, feel free to use anything." Her eyes were filled with tears as her mother hugged her. The next day she took her to the hospital for a check-up and was told that Ruth should remain in hospital around two months; she would be given proper treatment and discharged as soon as possible.

Three months later she was feeling much better and was very happy. Her mum never hit her or treated her badly and took great care of her. Her self esteem and confidence became high and she was convinced there was no-one like her mother.

One day Ruth's mum said, "Angel."
Ruth replied, "Yes, Mum?"
"Come here."

Ruth looked at her, wondering what was on her mind. "What do you want to be, what do you want to do with your life?"

"I want to be a midwife or a nurse," she replied.

Her mum laughed. She gave Ruth a letter and asked her to open it. Ruth eagerly opened the letter and found it was an admission letter into primary school. She jumped up and hugged her mother as she had given up hope of ever going to school but now she felt there was hope for the future.

The next day, Ruth's mum took her out to do some shopping; she bought her school bags, shoes, socks, a water bottle, biscuits and much more. They arrived home feeling tired and hungry so her mum prepared some food and after a hearty meal they caught up with some sleep.

The next day was Sunday. They came back from church and her mum brought out her uniform. Ruth was excited and promised her mum to justify her faith in her by eventually becoming a nurse or a midwife. The day went slowly. Ruth wished that morning would come as she was so excited about starting school.

The next day she had her shower, ate her breakfast and put on her smart new uniform and white socks. Her mum also made sure she had some biscuits and drinks and promised to bring her lunch.

As they entered the school premises, Ruth was feeling proud. She watched the other children running up and down, some shouting, others screaming. At eight o'clock they rang the bell and Ruth was told to line up with the other students for assembly. After the assembly she joined the others in class and was welcomed by the teacher. Her first day at school was fun and she was thrilled her mum had the money to educate her.

The first term was nearly over and all the students had to sit their exams. Ruth's mum paid for her daughter to have extra tuition and encouraged her to work harder. But Ruth was nervous on the day of the exams. She didn't think she would do well.

The teacher called everyone and gave them a paper with their grade. Ruth had come twenty-sixth out of thirty pupils in the class. She wasn't too despondent and was confident her mum would be satisfied with her efforts. When she got home, she showed her result to her mum. She was disappointed but could do nothing but told her daughter to work hard next time.

After the disappointing first exam results Ruth's mum got her a private teacher and her next result was very good compared to the first one. The extra tuition ensured that she continued to progress. Her exam result in secondary school was impressive and she was given a scholarship, which would take her through secondary school and on to university.

She couldn't wait to get home to tell her mother the good news but something very strange was to happen to her on the way. It started with a minor problem. She boarded the school bus and the conductor asked her for her fare. But when she put her hand in her pocket she found her money had gone.

Ruth searched in her school bag but still could not find the money, so she told the conductor to ask the driver to stop. The conductor started to shout: "Give me my money! You entered my bus without money, come on, pay me!"

A few minutes later, the conductor said to Ruth, "You are lucky, that man over there paid for you." She was amazed and turned round to look at the man but could not see his face.

"Thank you, sir," she said, but the man said nothing and merely nodded his head slightly. When he got off at the next stop Ruth looked back to see if she could see his face but he was nowhere to be seen.

Ruth returned home to find her mum looking sad. She told her all that happened on the way back from school then her mother looked at her with her eyes filled with tears and said, "It was your dad, he showed himself to you, your dad is dead. May his soul rest in peace. Amen." Later that day, Ruth met her half-brothers and sisters; they too were in tears, but Ruth felt nothing for her departed father.

Ruth's dad was a wealthy man but had also been very wicked. She thought about him and his deeds. Her memories of him were mostly ones she'd rather forget.

He was tall with a dark complexion and he was well educated. He was a surgeon in the military. But he was also known to worship idols. Everybody feared him as he was totally heartless.

He worshipped different idols such as the god of thunder; Orumila, Sango, the god of fire; Obgunegbu, the god of children. Every morning, he would take mashed yam, oil and peppers to his shrine then perform incantations and leave the food there. He would pour Ogogoro (spirit) at the face of the shrine each morning and each weekend he would kill a duck and pour the blood on the face of his idol then sing and dance.

On Sundays he would dress up in white and take a live goat, sometimes pregnant ones, to the river. He would also take with him peppers, salt, yam, plantains and other food items with him and meet other, like-minded people at the river. Then they would dance, perform incantations and throw all their gifts into the water. Ruth's friends, who were poor, would wait at the bank of the river. Once the idol worshippers had left, the children would dive into the river and bring all the food and sacrifices back home but, of course, the worshippers believed the goddess of the river has accepted their offerings.

Sometimes, childless women would go to Ruth's dad and plead with him to ask the goddess of the river to give them children. He would often oblige but the parents would end up having problems after the child had been born. What's more he would use anything that breathed to offer as a sacrifice. However, one thing that gladdened Ruth's heart was that before he died, her dad confessed all his sins and accepted Christ as his Lord and personal saviour. He gave his life to God and asked for a pastor. The pastor came and prayed for him until he had breathed his last breath. He was born again and was with God in Heaven.

One day, Ruth came back from school to find her mum was extremely ill. She was desperately afraid because she had never seen her in such a condition. She bent down next to her mother and asked what had happened, but she was unable to respond. Ruth began to panic and cry. She called for help but no one was around to help her. As she had often seen her mum try to revive patients when they were unconscious, she knew what to do and put her in the recovery position until eventually she began to breathe. From that day onwards her mum never fully regained her health but despite the setback she eventually returned to work and carried out her daily duties. Nevertheless, she went to see her doctor and underwent a series of tests. As it turned out they were negative so she decided to leave her problems in the hands of God.

Unfortunately, her illness continued for five years and still there was no sign of recovery. Then, late one night, she woke and began to scream. Ruth got up and found her mum in tears. She talked and tried to encourage her, but could tell from her behaviour that something was seriously wrong. Her mum gave her the impression that she knew something but was reluctant to say what it was but continued to advice Ruth. Ruth managed to calm her mother down, returned to her bed and fell asleep.

The next morning after preparing for school, Ruth woke her mother to give her a bath but found she was unable to get her out of bed. When she managed to help her to her feet she had difficulty in walking. Ruth carried her mother, who was becoming increasingly weak, to the bath and placed her in lukewarm water. After giving her a bath she dried her body and dressed her in clean clothes. Seeing just how ill her mother was, she decided not to go to school; it was clear to her that she needed to be cared for and that had to take priority. Ruth wrote a letter to her school, letting them know of her mum's illness and informing them that she would be absent from school until she recovered.

Things became worse and a few weeks later her mum couldn't even speak. Ruth tried to communicate with her but without success and finally in desperation she called her half sister, who lived in England, and told her all that had happened. She offered her words of encouragement and promised to send some money for her mum's treatment.

Ruth also went to her Aunt, Maggie. "I have no money to care for her," said her aunt, "but I'll come over and see what I can do to help." When she saw how ill she was Auntie Maggie suggested she should be taken to her home town Ara, in the heart of Del. Auntie Maggie is the older sister to Ruth's mum (Carole). Ruth disagreed with her and insisted her mum belonged at home and not in the village, where there would be no one to care for her. Her step-sister Faith agreed with Ruth's aunt and was adamant that it was better for her to die in the village so that her people could bury her rather than her die in the city, which would incur substantial funeral costs.

As soon as Ruth heard that, she was gripped with fear and ran to her mum, begging her to stay with her, because she was all she had left in the world. But her mother couldn't say a thing and Ruth suspected she wouldn't have done so had she been able.

Faith came to the house one morning and advised Ruth to consider a native doctor; she believed a native doctor would cure the illness and enable her mum to get better. Fortunately, there was a neighbour who specialised in such treatments. However, he stated that Ruth's mum was suffering from a very serious illness and that spiritual help was what she needed, not native medicine. But Faith insisted she should be treated by a native doctor, so he agreed to her wishes at a cost of 5,000 naira. He commenced the treatment immediately even though Ruth was aware that her mum did not like anything herbal. Nevertheless, she decided there was nothing she could do or say to stop them.

The next morning Faith rushed down to the house and shouted, "Get dressed, you have to take your mum to the village." Ruth was greatly alarmed by this sudden intrusion and began to cry and shake uncontrollably.

"What is it? Talk to me!" demanded Ruth.

"I saw your mum early this morning, she looked gravely ill. I called to her but she didn't answer."

Ruth was confused. "So what are you saying?"

Faith replied in a whisper, "Your mum… she's going to die. So you have to be fast."

Ruth was just 13 years old, with no family or friends to support her. Her whole world had been turned upside down; her hopes, ambitions, career and her love of life were slipping away. She cried to God to perform a miracle and heal her mum. Two days later, Auntie Maggie came with her belongings and asked Ruth to pack her things and her mum's clothes and they started the journey to Del.

They arrived at Ara at four in the afternoon. All the family were there to receive them, shocked at the sight of Ruth's mum. Immediately Auntie Maggie saw her family she began to cry and swear, and demanded her sister, Ruth's mum, be carried inside the house by the family. Uncle Ted asked her for the cause of her illness. "It's beyond medication," replied Ruth, "and she doesn't know what to do." Uncle Ted did his best to assure her that all would be well.

That afternoon all Carole's friends came to visit her but they were in for a shock. Aunt Maggie and Uncle Ted had called in a native, superstitious doctor to find out the cause of her illness. "This woman," claimed the doctor, "has offended the god of the land and sacrifices must be carried out in order to cleanse the curse. Her daughter Ruth will have to kneel down at the grave of her granddad to plead with his spirit so that her mum can be healed; also her mother has killed innocent babies including Ruth's late brother Judy."

At hearing this Ruth was in a state of shock. "My mum is a good Christian," she said, "and as night follows day my mum would not do such things because it is against God.

What's more, Ruth was unconvinced by what she was being asked to do. The Bible had taught her that men have authority over all demons on earth so why should she plead with a dead person? A person that has no life that cannot talk or hear or speak. So she cried, "Why should I beg this person to save her and do sacrifices for a god that cannot help, cannot see, cannot hear, and cannot speak?"

At this, the native doctor – or, more accurately, the juju man – shouted at her and told her to be calm or he would cast a curse on her, but Ruth continued, "The Bible also says that God will never curse his children, that he that dwells in the secret place, shall abide by the shadow of the almighty God and touch not his anointed and do his prophet no harm."

The juju man became angry and left. The family were furious with her for challenging the native doctor and speaking blasphemy against their gods. It had been a very challenging day for Ruth. She went up to her mum, prayed with her and told her everything would be fine.

Several days later she overheard her aunts and uncles talking about buying a casket for her mum and that she would die soon. On hearing that she ran to her mum and told her all she had heard. "Don't be afraid of death," her mother said, "because God gives life and just as surely he will take it away. When the time comes I will be happy in the knowledge that I am about to meet my redeemer." Ruth didn't understand and asked for an explanation but her mother just smiled.

One day her mum called Ruth and asked her to plait her hair. Ruth made her look pretty and her mother thanked her for her efforts. Then she made the rather odd comment that this was the popular hair style amongst women and soon she would be joining them.

Night came and the two of them prayed together. Later, Ruth had a dream: she was being flogged by a teacher when suddenly her mum appeared and told the teacher never to touch her again. When she woke up she looked at the time and saw it was five minutes to six in the morning. She ran to her mum's room, knelt down and spoke softly but her mother did not answer. She lifted her head and placed it on her legs and called out, "Mum, Mum, speak to me, what is it?"

She opened her eyes and said, "Pray, be strong, tell your sister I love her and never lose faith in God. Can you see them? They look so beautiful all in white, they are here for me, but now, Ruth, I have to go." She smiled at her daughter then took her last breath and died.

"Mum!" Ruth shouted, "Mum, speak to me, Mum, please don't leave me! Then she ran to tell her uncles, who came and tried to revive her but it was too late. She was dead.

Ruth was devastated. It seemed her world had come to an end. Her mother's body was taken away, bathed and put in the casket her brothers and sister had bought for her. She walked up to her uncles and aunts and said, "I suppose you'll all be happy now. Well, you can take away my mum and take away all that belonged to her but you can never take away her soul nor will you separate her from God!"

After she was buried, there was no hope of staying in the village. She told her mum's younger sister Auntie Hope, who had been very kind to her, she would be going back to Lag the next day. Auntie Hope took her to church that evening for prayers and Ruth left the village the next day for Lag.

After the death of her parents, Ruth, still only 13, lived alone in a one room apartment and was given financial assistance by a charity organisation (St Vincent de poor). She would wake up early each morning to prepare for school and during the break she would join her friends at the food vendor and eat their leftovers, while sometimes they buy her food.

Ruth's landlord wanted to marry her. She refused and as a result she was asked to move out of the property. Ruth had nowhere to go, nobody to turn to, except for God. She decided to borrow some money.

She called her half-sister, who was still living in England, and told her what had happened. She assured her that all would be well but nothing happened. Ruth was going through a difficult period with no money, she later moved in with her half sister where they shared a one room apartment, with Ruth selling pure water after school in order to survive. She had no choice but to sleep under the bridge, sometimes at home and sometimes outside in the kitchen. At night, some of the homeless children would join her and they would live as a family.

Ruth had a very good friend called John who she always referred to as 'J'. He came from a wealthy background and, having lost his mum when he was two months old but was raised by his stepmother and his dad. His dad was rarely at home while his step-mum was a full-time housewife, she treated him badly. She would call him a wizard and packed all his belongings to the guest room. J was only allowed to sleep in the guest kitchen as his stepmother said he was a pig and pigs don't sleep in clean environments. He would have to lay on a cloth on the ground, cold and uncomfortable. Sometimes he would have sleepless night thinking of his dead mum he never knew and wished he had died when his mum was giving birth to him.

One day J went to school and didn't return home because he couldn't cope with his stepmother no longer. He just wished his dad could see her for the wicked woman she really was.

Ruth's landlord tried every trick he could to marry her but she refused to accept his proposals. Then one night something strange happened. After her night's revision, she left her bedroom door open. About an hour later she felt someone touching her; she tried to open her eyes but couldn't. She began to scream but no one could hear her. She struggled with the intruder but he was very strong. Clearly, he was trying to rape her.

She struggled till she felt helpless but then noticed her pen which she used for schoolwork, on the bedside table. She quickly grasped it and used it to stab the man in his groin area. The room was dark so she could not tell who her assailant was but she watched him get up and groan in pain before quickly running out of the room.

Some weeks later after getting over the trauma of the incident, Ruth reflected on the fact that she had overcome the man and avoided being raped. She was saving her purity for her husband and it meant an awful lot to her. Some weeks after the incident she fainted and was taken to the hospital. The doctor said she was suffering from a stomach ulcer. She was told not to eat pepper for eighteen months so that her stomach could heal. That proved to be quite a punishment. She became very conscious of what she eats, although she had little or no food.

Several months later, her landlord came back yet again asking for her hand in marriage. She spoke about it to her half sister who she lives with. Her half sister told her to accept his proposal so that she would be left alone and not have to pay rent. It made no difference. She thought about it and rejected the offer. At this the landlord became furious and ordered her to leave his house, fortunately, Ruth half sister in London called her to instruct her to move in with her husband friend in Suru, God healed and answered, Ruth prayed at the time of her need.

Ruth was delighted, She began to pack immediately but was told to take just her clothes; she didn't understand as she didn't know why she was unable to take her mum's clothes with her. She gave some of her clothes to the poor in the church and some to married women who couldn't afford to clothe themselves. She gave her mum's medical equipment to her half brother to keep and she shared her mum's property remaining property among the poor and off she went. She got into a taxi and within an hour she was in Suru.

The bus conductors were shouting "Suru! Suru!" Everyone was busy and people were running around frantically. The taxi took a right turn and finally stopped in front of a tall building where she stepped out of the taxi. She then walked into the building, and reached a gate which was opened by a young lady. After a brief discussion she was welcomed and asked to enter.

The first few days were fun, but things soon began to change. The family with whom she lived with were Muslims which meant living there was very challenging as they only cater for themselves, cook their own food, buy their own food ingredients, toiletries, arrange their own transport to school etc. Occasionally, when the Muslim family were in a good mood, they would offer Ruth some food to eat or even money to take to school.

Ruth took care of herself although her half sister in London would sometimes send money and clothes; she would save the money for emergencies. She worked as a sales girl in a restaurant, her shifts starting at 5pm after school. It was a demanding schedule for a young lady at her age; she was offered dinner and 50 naira for her day's travel.

She would finish work at 3am, sleep for 3 hours and get ready for school. She constantly had pains in her joints and headache. Ruth would take Paracetamol to ease her pain; due to lack of funds she would normally have to go to bed in pain.

Ruth's half sister Julia who is based in England with her families is the first child of the family. Julia wanted Ruth to join her in England to help her care for her children and give her half sisters a better education. Julia called Ruth and advised her that their visas were now available and they would soon be joining her in London. Ruth was delighted.

Few days later, Ruth fell ill and was rushed to hospital where she had her appendix removed.

A NEW LIFE

Two weeks after her operation, the big day finally came with Ruth waving goodbye to all her friends and well-wishers. She was the happiest girl on earth. It was the first time she had travelled by air and it all seemed like a dream. She boarded the plane, which was clean and well furnished. In a strange way she felt she was in her father's living room. She was on the plane for six hours and finally reached her destination.

Julia and uncle D were waiting for her and her sister at the airport. "I'm so sorry about your mum," said Julia. "I wish I had been there to share your pain but at least you're safe now." They got into the car and drove off and arrived at her home in Ray, late that night. They were shown to their room, had a hearty meal and finally went to bed.

The next morning, Julia showed them the bathroom, kitchen, living room, toilet and the garden. When it was time for them to take their bath, Ruth made a silly mistake, she took the sponge used for cleaning the bath and used it to bath herself. After washing herself, she poured some toothpaste in the bath and washed the sink with it instead of using soap. When she was asked what she was using to wash the bath she said, "Colgate." Then Ruth realised Colgate was the name of a tooth paste and laughed about it. All this was new to her; she'd always lived in a city in Africa but had never come across the name Colgate.

Around two months after arriving in the UK, Ruth was in the kitchen when Simeon, Julia's husband came and asked, "Do you have a boyfriend?"

She was shocked. "No," she replied, "I'm only fifteen years old."

"Don't worry," he said. "You will have one very soon." Then he left her.

It was the first time he'd been alone with her. She wondered what he meant by 'very soon'. He continued to bother her, one day Ruth was washing the dishes, he came and patted her on her bum. She immediately turned and said to him, "I don't like what you just did."

But he just laughed and said, "You will get use to it." Once again he left her and she continued to wonder what he was up to. This went on for several weeks and Ruth was becoming scared. She couldn't tell her half sister Julia as she guessed she probably wouldn't believe her and probably beat her and send her packing.

Ruth was now even more scared. She would have willingly gone back to Africa but she didn't have any family back there, no one to help and support her. She couldn't go to her previous home address because her landlord wanted to have an affair with her. She was desperate and didn't know what to do.

She felt extremely bitter and tired of Simeon constant harassment. She was tired of living in fear, tired of living in a world seemingly full of sin and sinners. Ruth finally decided she wanted to put an end to it all, so she took an overdose of tablets. Before she did, she wrote a letter explaining why she had come to such an extreme decision.

But it didn't work out the way Ruth expected. She took the tablets and felt free, as though a weight had been lifted from her shoulders. It was all to no avail. She woke up the next morning to the realisation that her suicide attempt had failed and she began to cry.

Ruth had no choice but to carry on. Although she was in college doing her 'A' levels, she couldn't concentrate in class and would even fall asleep during lectures. Her tutor knew something wasn't right with her so he took her to see the school counsellor. She told the counsellor she was hungry and as a result he spoke to her head teacher who arranged for her to be put on daily lunch at school.

Despite this improvement in Ruth's circumstances things at home didn't change and Simon continued to sexually harass her. He would come to her room at night and put his hand over her mouth, saying things like, "Don't shout, if you do you are in trouble." Then he would force himself upon and thrust inside her over and over again until she could barely stand the pain. His behaviour was repulsive. He would stroke her breasts and thighs, insert his fingers in her private part and relieve himself in unimaginable ways, usually forcing Ruth to assist him until he was fulfilled. Sometimes he would come to her room, while she was fast asleep, and touch her under the blankets. She would wake up petrified, knowing her ordeal was about to begin once more. After one such occasion, Ruth again took an overdose thinking this would end her life but yet again she was unsuccessful. However, in spite of everything, she continued to believe that God had a plan for her.

One day, Simon went out with Julia and left the kids at home. About twenty minutes later, he came back home. Ruth was instantly afraid and asked him if he had forgotten something. But he said he hadn't.

He went inside his room and brought out a video cassette as Ruth ironed her little nephew's uniform. When he called and asked for a drink, Ruth went into the kitchen for a glass of water and took it into his room. But the drink was a trap to ensnare Ruth. He held her neck, pushed her into the living room and made her look at pornography that was being played on the TV. She told him she didn't want to watch it but he pressed her neck even harder. It was hopeless. Ruth had no choice but to watch because her neck was hurting.

"This is what your sister and I do," he said. "You will be joining us eventually."

Julia came home later in the evening. Ruth acted as though nothing was wrong, as though everything was ok. But alone in her bedroom she was full of thoughts she didn't know what to do.

Later that night he entered her bedroom and put his hand over her mouth, Ruth threatened to tell Julia.

He just laughed. "What on earth makes you think your sister would believe you? She would beat you and send you packing!" On hearing those words Ruth was quiet. Deep down she knew he was right.

He squeezed her breasts tightly and moved his hands down to her legs. She was shaking and begged him to stop. He merely continued and told her not be scared. Finally he removed his trousers, lifted up her skirt and her ordeal began once more. Later he left her room. By then she was shaking and crying and eventually fell asleep in tears.

The following morning Ruth had an idea. On her way from school the next day, she walked into Dix's electrical appliances store and bought a recorder. The assistant taught her how to use it.

Later that evening, Simon whispered to Ruth that he would be coming to her room, Ruth did not appear frightened as usual instead she shrugged her shoulders and walked away. At night fall, he knocked on her door, Ruth started the tape recorder and opened the door. He wanted to touch her and she told him to stop. She threatened him by saying she would call the police but he refused to stop. Everything he said to her was recorded on the tape and he finally left. She continued to record the event on two more occasions.

But in spite of the evidence she had accumulated Ruth was still afraid to go to the police as she feared what her sister and her husband Simeon would do to her.

One day she arrived home from school and found there was no one at home. She felt relieved at being alone in the house and took off her clothes to have a shower. Her feeling of security was short lived as Simon walked in just as she had undressed. She covered herself up with her towel and begged him to leave her room but he refused. Ruth was terrified. She stepped back till there was no more room. He moved towards her and took her in his arms. She struggled and tried to push him away but he was too powerful. After much protest he overpowered her. He pulled off his shorts and lay on top of her then she screamed and shouted for help but no-one came.

When he had finished he looked down and apologised for what he had done but left Ruth in tears as he walked away. She wished the earth would open up and swallow her; she wished she had never come to England; she wished she was dead. She was so depressed that she took yet another overdose, but again to no avail.

Yet, Ruth clung on to the belief that God is good and that God wanted her to live because he had a plan for her. Nevertheless, despite her predicament she couldn't tell anyone because she was afraid no-one would believe her and she would end up in Africa.

One thing Ruth did right from the first day Simon started abusing her was to keep a diary of all that has been happening. She decided it would be a good idea to have a record of what was being done to her and how often. A few days later, he came to her again, this time at four in the morning, Julia was at home with the kids, Ruth began to scream; unfortunately, Julia didn't come to her aid.

However, the following morning Ruth summoned up the courage to talk to her sister about what had happened during the night and she was amazed at the way she reacted.

"I'm sorry," said Julia, "for my husband's behaviour. He had no right to do that to you.

Ruth was shocked although she said little and went to school that day as normal. When she returned at four in the afternoon Julia was furious and told her the police came to the house earlier in the day.

"Why did you have to go and report us!" she screamed.

"But I didn't report you," replied Ruth, "I don't know what you're talking about. Julia didn't believe her

What neither of them knew, however, was that during the morning a neighbour had heard Ruth screaming and gone to the police. Ruth went to school the next day, she couldn't concentrate in class, she later went to see the school counsellor but she didn't disclose her ordeal. Later that afternoon, she was called by the school child protection officer where everything came out in the open.

Eventually, she was taken away from the house by the police and the social services and was put in an hostel. Ruth was confused, scared and ashamed. At times she thought that God had deserted her. Her life was almost as miserable as the life she'd left behind but it was the best she could hope for. One of her fellow inmates was a heroin addict and Ruth was terrified she might be drawn into the lifestyle.

One morning at three o' clock, she saw the inmate lying by the door. There was a man standing next to her, "She's dead," he said gravely. "We've just called for an ambulance."

Later the police came to the hostel to take some statements, while Ruth explained she could not sleep in her room that night so she was taken to a friend's place where she spent the night.

She contacted the social services again and they were concerned about Ruth's new situation. Ruth requested to move from her present hostel and her request was granted. She was moved to another area of south east where she lived for two months and was later transferred to the Ele area. Life in the Ele was challenging but she was determined to make it work. She managed to enter college and continue her education, she continued and believed God in her situation.

After going through thick and thin in the hostel, Ruth was finally given a place of her own in a large, peaceful environment. It was a far cry from being in the hostel, where girls would smoke, drink, quarrel, scream and fight.

Things were to get even better. She eventually gained a place on a degree course. Things were improving all the time and all the while Ruth continued to believe God had a plan for her.

EPILOGUE

Ruth had lived a miserable existence and the memories of her childhood continued to hurt her and give her nightmares, but she encourages herself "life must go on come what may".

Nevertheless, nothing could ever erase or change what had happened. It was a scar she would have to live with for the rest of her life. She had tried to kill herself on three separate occasions but God had not allowed her to die.

By this time Ruth no longer trusted a man sufficiently to go into a relationship or go close. Her experiences had led her to believe that men were equally untrustworthy.

Her family wanted her to drop the sexual charges, She was threatened several times but she was more determined to see justice been done. Ruth made a friend Kev in church, he was like a brother to her and kept in constant touch to see how she was. There was something about him that she couldn't quite explain. Whatever it was, Ruth was happy but have reservation.

Ruth attended court hearings, She had no support from her family, she was castigated and had no one to comfort her. Her friends from church were there, they stood by her, believed her, and became her only family

Ruth appeared in court twice to give evidence, after several days of hearing in the court of justice Simon was found guilty. In spite of everything, Ruth forgave him and she left it to God to decide upon his judgement. Furthermore, she would often pray for her family, hoping that things will get better.

Despite all Ruth had been through, she never lost faith in God nor did she lose hope, as she believed that all things are possible for God. Indeed, she actually felt as though she had become closer to God. She engaged herself in cell meetings and prayer meetings. Going to court had been a great ordeal for her but she accepted it because she was convinced God had a plan for her. She felt no bitterness towards those who had persecuted her as she was guided by the words of the Bible "Vengeance is mine says the Lord".

Throughout the difficult times, God had been there for her, she had never been alone. He had guided her all the way. Ruth had found peace in God; he had blessed her and given her understanding; he had blessed her kindness; he had filled her heart with gladness and, finally, happiness.

Ruth's wants to be closer to God more than before. God has said he will prepare a table before her in the presence of her enemies; that was why he never let her alone so that he can accomplish his word (Psalm 23). He strengthened her, gave her life when she thought she was lifeless; he gave her hope when there was none; he gave her joy when she was in sorrow; and he was always with her. God never left her for a second. He had always been there for her.

Upon all her trials in life Ruth with the help of her friend's, church and God was able to complete her degree and master degree and now married to a wonderful man, blessed with a child.

Although she is not in good terms with her family but she is very happy.

She was never alone.